101 WAYS TO GET STRAIGHT A's

Robin Dellabough

Illustrations by Barbara Levy

Troll Associates

ACKNOWLEDGMENTS

This book could not have been written without the help of students, parents, and teachers. Many thanks to the following students at Irvington Middle School and Irvington High School: Joe Adelman, Rumeli Banik, Jeff Berman, David Birrittella, Ben Chandler, Emily Gold, Jacob Grose, Kayoko Hoshi, Juliet Kiel, Carly Lichtenstein, Wendy Liu, Sarika Malhotra, Emily Neiditch, Shana Neiditch, Deepa Ranganathan, Hugh Ryan, Misaki Samejima, Siddharth Sawkar, Josh Shaevitz, Nicole Slavin, Elisabeth Snell, Peter Tavolacci, Chris Wong, Elana Wolff, and Gabby Zeitchick.

Special appreciation goes to teachers Judy McQuistion, Lisa Urban, Chuck Johnson, Robert Hubertus, Jody Grose, Bruce Carlsten, and most especially, Barbara Whitehill.

Parents and their children who took time to talk with me include Ariel and Gail Bulua; Pam and Lauren Petlick; Lea and Colin Richardson; Jon, Flynn, and Joel Berry.

Text and illustrations copyright © 1994 by Troll Associates, Inc.

All rights reserved. No part of this book may be used or reproduced in any manner whatsoever without written permission from the publisher.

Printed in the United States of America.

10 9 8 7 6

For Brian's children
Elona and Keegan Gormley

Contents

CHAPTER 1

Who Cares? Why *You* Care!

Would you like your very next report card to be better than your last one? If you picked up this book you have already taken the first step. Maybe you really want to try for straight A's. Maybe you want to see how much you can improve your grades, even from C's to straight B's. No matter what your goal, you can get better grades.

This book will show you how. It's divided into chapters according to people you relate to as a student, starting with the most important person: yourself.

You may not have the power to get straight A's every marking period. But you definitely have the power to do better than you're doing now. These pages are crammed with tips from other successful students, helpful teachers, and even a few parents!

You don't have to try all 101 suggestions. Just pick a few at a time and see how they work for you. We can't guarantee straight A's, but we promise you will get more out of school—the place you spend hours of your life!

Good grades pay off in lots of ways you can't even imagine yet. Getting straight A's in middle school may not seem like a big deal, but it helps you to:
• Feel great about yourself
• Give you enough confidence to try new experiences
• Lay the groundwork for going to the best college
• Save you and your family money through scholarships
• Give you many more choices in life
• Best of all, when you work toward straight A's it means you're learning—and isn't that what school's all about?

Learning puts you ahead after you get out of school, too. You may have heard about the global economy. More and more, the world is becoming one big marketplace. So whether you become a scientist or a stockbroker, you need both skills and education to keep up with workers around the world.

So...ready for your first way to get straight A's?

Study Habits of the Rich and Famous

Did You Know...

Science fiction author **Isaac Asimov** checked out a book from the library every two days.

Magic Johnson, one of the greatest basketball players ever, played on a basketball team in fifth grade that lost only one game—when Magic's teacher forbid him to play because he didn't turn in an assignment.

Booker T. Washington, former slave and college founder, was 11-years-old by the time he convinced his stepfather to let him go to school. He still had to work from 4 AM to 9 AM and then for two hours after school.

Horror writer **Stephen King** read all the time as a student. Some of his favorite authors were Thomas Hardy, Jack London, Ken Kesey, J.R.R. Tolkien, and Margaret Mitchell.

Sandra Day O'Connor, the first woman Supreme Court Justice, lived with her grandmother so she could go to a private school. She did so well she skipped a grade. When she was home on her parents' ranch, she read a lot of the newspapers and magazines that her parents subscribed to, including *National Geographic, Wall Street Journal, Los Angeles Times,* and the *Saturday Evening Post.*

Florence Griffith-Joyner, Olympic track star, set goals for herself in a diary she kept. She also enjoyed reading poetry.

Inventor **Thomas Edison's** mother taught him mathematics, geography, history, and English at home and always encouraged him to do his best.

Civil rights leader **Martin Luther King, Jr.** advanced so far ahead of his class through his reading that he skipped ninth and twelfth grades.

Jacques Cousteau, ocean explorer, wrote, illustrated, and mimeographed a book when he was 13.

Theodore Roosevelt, 26th United States President, loved to read adventure novels and books about Africa and the West. He started our National Parks system.

Cable television network head **Ted Turner** read a book a week.

Benjamin Franklin, statesman and one of our country's founders, had trouble with math until he made up math games and raised his grades.

Albert Einstein's teachers didn't believe he was that smart. Fortunately his parents encouraged him and helped him to become a true genius and receive a Nobel Prize.

CHAPTER 2

You and Your Mind: First Things First

1. The key to straight A's is knowing why you want good grades. Students and teachers say the more specific your reasons, the more likely you are to succeed. Think about why you want an A. Is it because:
- You want to please your parents?
- You want to get into a good college?
- You want to impress your friends?
- You want to prove to yourself that you can do it?
- You want to take an honors course in a subject you like?
- You want to qualify for a scholarship?
- You want to go to a special summer program?
- You want to go to a private school?
- You want to be able to tell your own children you got straight A's when you were in school?

Now write down each reason that applies to you. You'll be even more motivated if you can read your own goals every now and then.

2. Once you know why you want a great report card, PAY ATTENTION. Every top student says that's the quickest way to straight A's.

- Catch yourself if you start daydreaming in class.
- Take good notes.
- If you get bored, remind yourself of your goals.
- It's easier to pay attention if you can sit up front. Teachers usually are happy to change your seat.
- During desperately boring moments, pinch yourself (but don't scream out loud).

3. Did you ever think about how you learn? Most people have a certain learning style. The three main ways to learn are *auditory, visual,* and *kinesthetic*. To take advantage of your personal style, first you need to figure out what it is.

If you're auditory, you do best when you HEAR information. Then you can:

- Understand and follow lectures easily.
- Take notes as you listen.
- Listen to tapes of books.
- Read essays aloud to yourself or to someone else.
- Read into a tape recorder and play it back. Hearing your own voice is very effective.

If you're visual, you do best when you SEE information. You need to:

- Read material.
- See an illustration.
- Draw diagrams or charts of the subject.
- Use different-colored highlighters.
- Make flashcards.
- Watch educational TV, documentaries, and videos.

If you're kinesthetic, you do best when you DO something. You:

- Excel at hands-on projects.
- Need to choose dioramas, posters, sculptures, or dances whenever possible.
- Learn by role-playing, building, or performing.
- Memorize well while juggling or skipping rope.
- Can knit, sew, or crochet while studying.

4. No matter which learning style you use, the best students read all the time. There is a direct link between how much you read and your grades. Utilize your free time by either reading newspapers, magazines, books, comics, or skimming encyclopedias and dictionaries.

Notes on Notes

Taking good notes will make studying for tests and writing reports much easier. The trick is to stick with a SYSTEM that works for you. You may have to vary the system from teacher to teacher, according to their lecture styles.

- Use your own shorthand. Examples:

  Leve ot som vwls. Yu'll b amzd at hw mch yu cn stll undrstnd.

  Use just the beginning letters of each word (eng for English, sci for science, w for with)

  Drop the endings of -ing or -tion words (end for ending)

  Try abbreviations (PM for afternoon, W for West)

  Draw symbols (& for and, = for equals, > for more than, CO_2 for carbon dioxide)
- Be sure you WRITE CLEARLY enough to read your notes later.
- Leave plenty of room on each page of notes and between lines to fill in information you may want to add.
- Recopy or type your notes to reinforce your memory.
- Underline or highlight the important phrases or points.

You know you're over-highlighting when you mark almost everything.

•Pay attention to clues your teacher gives you while taking notes. When you hear something like, "What I've been saying for the last ten minutes really sums up this month's whole unit," star those notes to study thoroughly for the next test.

Here are examples of different ways to take notes.

Formal Outline
The Human Body
I. Bones
A. Give shape to body
B. Kinds of bones
1. Short
a. feet
b. wrists
2. Long
a. legs
b. arms
c. fingers
3. Flat
a. ribs
b. shoulder blades
II. Skin
A. Protects body from injury, water loss, or infection
B. Composed of two major layers
1. Epidermis or outer layer of cells
a. hair
b. nails
c. sweat glands
2. Dermis or inner layer
a. nerves
b. blood vessels

III. Muscles
   A. Allow body to move
   B. More than 650 types
      1. Skeletal
      2. Cardiac
      3. Smooth

Informal Outline

The Human Body
consists of many different parts
1. Bones
   —give shape
   —short
      —feet, wrists
   —long
      —legs, arms, fingers
   —flat
      —ribs, shoulder blades
2. Skin
   —protects body from injury, water loss, or infection
   —composed of two major layers
      —epidermis or outer layer
        -hair, nails, sweat glands
      —dermis or inner layer
        -nerves, blood vessels
3. Muscles
   —allow body to move
   —more than 650 types
      —skeletal
      —cardiac
      —smooth

17

Key Words

The Human Body

Consists of bones, muscles, ligaments, skin, cells, viscera

Bones give shape to body

Short bones are feet, wrists

Long bones are legs, arms, fingers

Flat bones are ribs and shoulder blades

Skin protects body from injury, water loss, or infection

Composed of two major layers

Epidermis is the outer layer of cells like hair, nails, sweat glands

Dermis is inner layer of tissue consisting of nerves and blood vessels

Muscles allow body to move

There are more than 650 types of muscle including skeletal, cardiac, and smooth

5. Be involved! That means being interested in world events, community affairs, and, especially, what's happening in your own classroom. By participating in class, you prove to yourself and your teachers you really do understand and are learning. That adds up to more A's.

6. Talk to yourself! Give yourself messages such as "I know I can do well on this report," or "Good job." Positive self-talk can make the difference between a B+ and an A. It also boosts your self-confidence, which is always good for grades.

7. Reward yourself after you've worked for a certain period of time. Small rewards such as taking a shower, making a snack, calling a friend, or watching TV can have big results in terms of motivation.

8. Some experts suggest that you stick to a set schedule. However, according to our student and teacher experts, sometimes it's easier to stay motivated if you vary your routine every now and then. On a beautiful day, read in the park; or during a blizzard, study next to a crackling fire.

9. Make up a silly new word or sentence out of the first letters of a list of words you need to memorize. Or learn the acronyms your teacher uses. To remember the planets in our solar system, for example:
  - My Very Educated Mother Just Served Us Nine Pizzas (Mercury, Venus, Earth, Mars, Jupiter, Saturn, Uranus, Neptune, Pluto).

10. Remember how easy it was to learn the alphabet by singing your ABC's? Make up songs to memorize complicated material. Or use rhymes such as "In fourteen-hundred and ninety-two, Columbus sailed the ocean blue."

11. Can Mozart make you smarter? Many straight-A students say listening to music clears their minds. Some teachers have shown that classical music with $4/4$ timing and 60 beats per minute can improve concentration and memory.

Mindmaps, Bubbles, Venn Circles, and Fishbones

If your learning style is mainly visual, these **graphic organizers** can help you memorize facts for tests, organize information for reports, and see how a chapter fits together.

Mindmap

In mindmapping, you draw pictures of the subject and label them with facts. Here's an example of a mindmap a 10-year-old boy made for a unit on the Middle Ages.

Bubbles

You try to put just one idea in each bubble and then see how they relate. This is a bubble graphic to describe clouds.

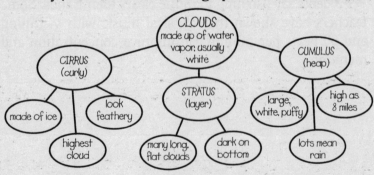

20

Venn Circles

You've probably used this kind of diagram for math problems. But here is an example of a way you can use it to organize a geography report.

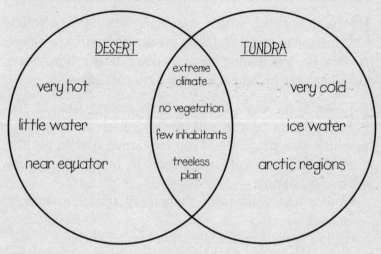

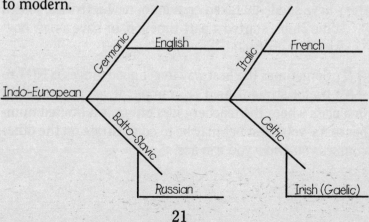

Fishbones

Like a family tree, fishbone maps help you see how different branches of information are connected. This fishbone is about the development of languages, from ancient to modern.

21

12. Colorful markers, jazzy pens, special notebooks, mechanical pencils—any equipment you especially love—help you stay "up" for school. And that means better grades. It's worth splurging on supplies once in awhile.

13. Switch tasks when you start getting frustrated. Instead of quitting, take a break from writing a report to work on the bibliography or cover illustration. Soon you'll be ready to get back to the hard part again.

14. Don't get lazy! If you've been getting straight A's, don't assume you will *always* get an A, no matter how little you study. Once you've learned how to get A's, keep up all those great study habits. Be on the grade-alert in these situations:
- You've just gone from elementary school to middle school.
- You've gone from middle school to high school.
- You've been moved up into an accelerated or honors class.
- You're switching from one school to another, for example, from a public school to a private school or from a school in a rural town to one in a large city.
- You've suddenly taken on a lot of new activities, joined some clubs, started a part-time job, or have a new boyfriend or girlfriend.

15. Sometimes the best way to get good grades is NOT to try for straight A's. For example, if you're struggling in a class where the teacher gives out only a limited number of A's, your best bet may be to concentrate on the other courses you *know* you can ace.

My Personal Way to Get Straight A's

Use this form to keep a record of your grades and goals.

English
Last marking period I got:_____
This marking period
  I want to get:_____
I will do this by using these tips
from *101 Ways to Get Straight
A's:* #___ #___ #___ #___ #___

Math
Last marking period I got:_____
This marking period
  I want to get:_____
I will do this by using these tips
from *101 Ways to Get Straight
A's:* #___ #___ #___ #___ #___

Social Studies
Last marking period I got:_____
This marking period
  I want to get:_____
I will do this by using these tips
from *101 Ways to Get Straight
A's:* #___ #___ #___ #___ #___

Science
Last marking period I got:_____
This marking period
  I want to get:_____
I will do this by using these tips
from *101 Ways to Get Straight
A's:* #___ #___ #___ #___ #___

Foreign Language
Last marking period I got:_____
This marking period
  I want to get:_____
I will do this by using these tips
from *101 Ways to Get Straight
A's:* #___ #___ #___ #___ #___

Art
Last marking period I got:_____
This marking period
  I want to get:_____
I will do this by using these tips
from *101 Ways to Get Straight
A's:* #___ #___ #___ #___ #___

Music
Last marking period I got:_____
This marking period
  I want to get:_____
I will do this by using these tips
from *101 Ways to Get Straight
A's:* #___ #___ #___ #___ #___

CHAPTER 3

You and Your Mind: Test It!

16. Paying attention in class, doing homework, studying effectively, and memorizing should make you well-prepared for any test. "Cramming" for tests would never be necessary in the best of all possible worlds. According to teachers, however, students do not live in this world. So they suggest that you study a little bit at a time, beginning three or four days before T-day. That way you won't stay up half the night and be too tired to do your best on the test.

17. As soon as you get the test, write down on the back or on scrap paper all the facts or acronyms you've memorized so you won't forget them if you need them. (You also won't be cluttering up your brain with unnecessary information if you don't.)

18. On objective tests (multiple choice, true/false, matching), **always** answer all the questions you're sure of first. Then you'll know how much time you have left to spend on the tougher questions.

Timely Test Tips

- Write down exactly WHEN and WHERE the test will be given in your assignment notebook. Post the date in your room or study area.
- Listen in class to any clues your teacher may give as to the test's content.
- Explain to your teacher before the test that you really want to do well. Ask for specific studying hints. One teacher gave a student who did this five essay questions and told her that three of them would be on the test.
- Begin studying at least three nights before the test.
- DO NOT stay up late the night before the test.
- Eat a super good breakfast the morning of the test.
- Bring lots of sharpened pencils, pens, a calculator, and any other necessary materials. Pack them the night before.
- Allow yourself plenty of time so you don't arrive for the test rushed and nervous.
- Take a deep breath once you receive the test. Close your eyes for a second. Tell yourself you're going to do well.
- If it's a standardized test, the kind with little circles to fill in, place the test to your left and the answer sheet to your right (if right-handed). Do the opposite if you're left-handed.
- Keep checking to see that your answers are lined up with the correct questions. It's easy to skip an answer line on this type of test.
- Think carefully. Think calmly.
- If you finish before time's up, go back over your answers. Studies have shown that your first guess is not neces-

sarily the right answer.

- When you get the test back, BE SURE to look it over thoroughly. Fill in the correct answers and use it as a study sheet for final exams.
- KEEP the test for future reference.
- Reward yourself with a treat. You finished another test. Well done!

19. As you're going through a test, mark with a check or star the problems you need to come back to or double-check if you're not sure of the answer. In the past, educators recommended that students go with their first choice. Recent research has shown that when a student changes an answer, the second one is usually correct.

20. When in doubt, guess—IF you're certain that only correct answers will be tallied for the final test score.

21. On subjective tests (essay questions or short answers), TAKE YOUR TIME. Pay special attention to the verbs your teacher uses. Are you supposed to compare, contrast, discuss, list, analyze, or describe? Underline these key words. Then keep checking back to make sure you're comparing and not listing, for example.

22. Think through what you want to say and then what order you need to say it in. Jot down a rough outline or key ideas you want to cover. If you run out of time, at least your teacher will see the direction you were going in and may give you some credit.

23. Make the first, or *topic,* sentence clear, concise, and strong. Then support it with details in the rest of the essay.

24. Spend time on the very last sentence. Make it more than a conclusion: make it so memorable and fresh that your teacher will come away impressed—just at the moment he or she is determining your grade.

25. When you absolutely do not know the answer, be creative. One student wrote on a test, "Although I don't know who discovered Cuba, I know that Amerigo Vespucci explored the South American coast and that America was named after him." The teacher gave him half credit!

26. Whenever you have a choice in book reports or term papers, choose a subject you feel strongly about. When you are passionate about your subject, you're more likely to get an A.

PATH TO PERFECT PAPERS

The Planning Forest
- Choose the most interesting topic you can think of
- Gather background information to make sure there are enough sources: skim reference books, look through card catalog, consult *Reader's Guide to Periodical Literature*
- Narrow down your topic
- Write one sentence that describes what your paper will be about—your THESIS Statement
- Begin taking notes—short facts, words, phrases, dates IN YOUR OWN WORDS on separate index cards
- Summarize, paraphrase, or quote on each card
- Organize your notes—sort index cards into similar categories, use different-colored cards for subtopics, create a short outline, check against your original thesis statement, check to see whether you need additional research
- Check with your teacher to see if you're on the right track

The Writing Mountain
- Review all your notes
- Use your thesis statement, changing it if necessary, to write your introduction
- Use your outline to arrange your subtopic index cards in the right order
- Turn each card into a complete sentence
- Repeat this process until you have used up all your index cards
- Write a strong conclusion

Revision Fields

- Read your paper to yourself
- Read it to someone else
- Decide if you have written the kind of paper your teacher wants
- Check its organization for logic
- Check your writing style for smooth flowing ideas and paragraphs that connect by transitional words
- Rewrite if necessary (for A papers, it's almost always a good idea)

Proofreading/Publishing Plains

- Proofread for spelling, grammar, and punctuation
- Write, type, or word process your final copy as carefully as possible
- Put your report in an attractive cover with a title page
- Add maps, graphs, other visual aids or illustrations

Picnic in the Meadow

- Break open a picnic basket and bask in the warm glow of receiving an A for your tough hike!

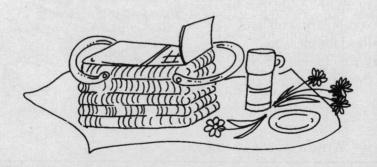

27. The single best way to turn a B paper into an A paper is to **REWRITE REWRITE REWRITE**. Although this takes practice and discipline, the more drafts you do, the better your writing will be. It's that simple.

• Ask someone you trust to read your first or second draft and make comments.

• Read your paper aloud to yourself. You won't believe how many mistakes you'll catch.

• Think of your writing as a garden. You need to weed out every unnecessary word. Then your thoughts will stand out like brightly colored flowers. Words that can almost always be deleted: very, really, nice.

28. There's no such thing as a day without homework for straight A students. Even if you don't have any assignments due the next day, spend some time on each academic subject. As little as ten minutes a day for each subject can add up to a better grade. Use the extra time to:

• Review and rewrite notes
• Start research on a project
• Outline textbook chapters as a test review
• Make up variations of math problems or vocabulary sentences
• Read for pleasure
• Write in your journal or a letter to a friend

SQ3R 4 U

SQ3R is *not* a new *Star Wars* droid—SQ3R stands for Survey, Question, Read, Recite, Review. It's a famous way to study textbooks (well, teachers think it's pretty hot stuff). If you really want to get straight A's, you will want to memorize this study system. And use it!

1. **SURVEY:** You skim the whole chapter assigned, looking for headings, summaries, outlines, and the order in which material is presented. This gives you a general idea of how the chapter is organized.

2. **QUESTION:** You try to answer questions about what you are reading, either by making up your own based on class lectures or general knowledge, or by using questions provided right in the book.

3. **READ:** Next you read the chapter carefully, trying to answer the questions you've thought of in step 2.

4. **RECITE:** You write down or say aloud your answers.

5. **REVIEW:** You go back and reread parts of the chapter to make sure your answers are accurate, to underline or take notes of especially important material, and to reinforce your memory.

CHAPTER 4

You and Your Time: It's On Your Side

29. WRITE IT DOWN. Make or buy an assignment pad or notebook. The difference between an A and a B is remembering to study for that math quiz on Thursday—because you wrote it down!

30. Get a big, expandable, cardboard file at the beginning of each school year. Stash ALL your tests and papers in it for easy review. Be sure to write the date on each assignment.

31. Post your class schedule in your locker, in a notebook, and at home. That way, you'll always know where you're supposed to be—and when!

32. Do you use the crumple-and-toss method of organization? Or are you the fold-and-forget in a book type? Try a pocket folder for each subject. Use one side for completed work and the other side for work to be done. Label each folder with subject AND order of schedule (first period, second period, etc.). Color code pocket folders with book covers for each subject. For example, science could all be red, math all green, English all blue.

33. Keep your backpack close to you at all times. Pretend it's another part of your body. At least twice a day, check it for homework, important notes, books, keys, garbage. As soon as you complete assignments, put them in your backpack so you'll never "forget" your homework again.

34. Do you get a new backpack every fall? Here's a neat way to recycle old backpacks AND keep your schoolwork organized. Each June, stash the previous year's papers, tests, report cards, and other special stuff in the backpack you're going to "retire." You'll have a colorful, convenient storage system.

HELP WITH HOMEWORK

This is a handy checklist for daily assignments.

DATE _____

Homework subjects:
__English   __math   __science
__foreign language __social studies

I need:
__paper   __graph paper   __pencils
__dictionary   __pens   __textbook
__markers   __workbook   __calculator
__ruler

I need to check with homework buddy: __Yes   __No

I need to do assignments in this order (hardest to easiest):
_____   _____
_____   _____
_____   _____

I have these extra activities today:
__sports practice __music lesson   __sports game
__job   __club meeting   __dance lesson
__other

I have put all assignments in my backpack: __Yes __No

---

35. Make the most of your natural "biorhythm." If you're a morning lark, get up early to study. If you think better at night, allow for after-dinner study time. If you get sleepy after dinner, study after school. It's better to go with the flow than to fight your own cycle.

36. Do you waste a lot of time worrying about how long homework is going to take? Put a time limit on how long you're going to work on each assignment. Knowing you *have* to stop at a certain point actually makes you more productive. Also, try plunging in for a very short time each day. Then gradually increase your study period. It's painless, and it really works. Soon you'll be able to concentrate for three times as long as you used to.

37. Do you have a problem with putting off work? The first step in putting an end to procrastination is to figure out exactly when you're studying and when you're not. Write down how long you spent on each subject. This means if you start writing a book report, but then get up to get a snack or fall asleep or start chasing your little brother around the house, you only count the time you were actually writing or thinking about the book. Keep track for a few weeks. You'll be amazed at the results.

38. Figure out your hardest assignment and get it out of the way while your mind is fresh. Not only will you do it more efficiently, the rest of your homework will seem like a breeze in comparison.

39. Have a project due in three weeks? Plan ahead. Get out your trusty assignment pad and break the project into small chunks. Create a schedule by working backwards from the due date to figure out how much you need to accomplish each day.

40. Keep your study area at home as neat as possible. You'll think more clearly, find supplies more easily AND save time.

41. Always have the right supplies handy so you don't waste energy in frustration. At the beginning of each semester, check your supplies against the list on page 77. Keep duplicate supplies in school and at home.

Long-Range Project Planner

Use this step-by-step approach for all projects that will take more than two weeks.

PROJECT: Book Report   ASSIGNED: Oct. 3   DUE: Nov. 4

By October 6

Choose type of book. Check with teacher for approval. Go to library.

By October 14

Start reading book. Write down questions and important notes as I read.

By October 18

Read at least up to page 55 (half the book).

By October 24

Finish reading whole book.

By October 31

Write rough draft. Ask Mom or Dad to read it and give comments.

By November 3

Finish final draft. Write or type it neatly. Get report cover.

TURN IT IN ON TIME!

42. Use summer vacations to:
- Get a headstart on reading for the next school year.
- Do some reading or research on a subject you love but never have enough time to learn about during school.
- Take a summer enrichment course. (See page 87 for a list of programs.) Guidance counselors say such courses "enhance" your college applications.

43. When planning your study space, remember your best learning style.
- If you're visual, keep the area clear of overly stimulating art, lights, mobiles, etc.
- If you're auditory, make sure it's quiet enough.
- If you're kinesthetic, it helps to have room enough to do a few jumping jacks.

Weekly Assignments

If your teachers give you assignments for the whole week, a weekly planner is essential. Here are samples of how two

DATE___April 25_____

WEEKLY HOMEWORK ASSIGNMENTS

	English	Math	Science	Social Studies	Spanish
Monday	Read Call of the Wild	Problems p. 60	Read Chap. 12	Start South America unit	Vocab words
Tuesday	Review questions	p. 65		Get research topic approved	
Wednesday			Lab		Quiz
Thursday				Start report	
Friday	Quiz		Test		Do play in Spanish
Reports	Book report due May 14			Report due June 1	

students with the same assignments filled in their weekly homework planner. Guess which student gets straight A's!

DATE_ April 25 ·

WEEKLY HOMEWORK ASSIGNMENTS

	English	Math	Science	Social Studies	Spanish
Monday	Read Call of the Wild— Chap. 2 & 3 (take notes)	p. 60—Do problems #10-25	Read p. 101-111 Answer questions on p. 112	Bring in any articles on South America	Study all vocabulary words on p. 25
Tuesday	Bring Call of the Wild to class prepared to discuss	p. 65 #1-10 (skip #3)		Get research topic approved	Memorize verb tenses for quiz tomorrow
Wednesday	Review questions #1-4		Bring in vinegar and baking soda for lab experiment	Go to library (research)	Quiz
Thursday	Study Chap. 1-3 for quiz (questions at end of chap.)		Turn in lab notes—study for test p. 95-111. Review last quiz	Read Chap. 6	Do oral presentation of Don Quixote
Friday	Quiz	Rewrite equations using diff. numbers for test next week	Test!!! (includes lab work)	Start rough draft	No class today! Teacher going to Spain!
Reports	May 14: Book report on book from same historical period— 3-4 pages			June 1: Research report on South American country 5-8 pages	

CHAPTER 5

You and Your Body: Home of Your Brain!

44. You've heard it before: eat breakfast! And we don't mean toaster-pastries, donuts, or even granola bars, all of which have tons of sugar, fat, and not much else. Your brain will work better if it is fueled by *protein*. A fifth-grader said, "I get hungry when I don't eat a good breakfast. I get restless and can't focus on anything in school."

Here are some quick and easy, high-protein breakfast ideas that will help you make it through a whole morning of school without dreaming of lunch:

- Yogurt with wheat germ, chopped nuts, and dried fruit
- Grilled cheese sandwich on wheat bread
- Peanut butter spread on frozen whole-grain waffles. Top with jam, syrup, banana slices, or apple butter
- Cinnamon raisin bagels with ricotta cheese

Get creative with last night's leftovers zapped in a

microwave for breakfast. Some foods taste even better the next day! (One A+ student says she eats pizza many mornings.)

Don't forget good old cereal. But choose high-protein, low-sugar kinds. Some good bets: Shredded Wheat, Special K, Cheerios, or Nutri-Grain.

45. Eat less junk food, sweet soda, or candy at lunch to stay wide awake during those afternoon classes. It may seem as if sugary snacks pump up your energy, but beware! The boost is only temporary. When the sugar wears off, you'll feel even more tired than before. Instead snack on high-energy foods like nuts, dried fruit, yogurt, bagels, cheese, or crackers. They stay in your body longer and give you a steadier stream of energy.

46. Avoid caffeine, the stuff in coffee, chocolate, cola-flavored soda, and tea. A bright 8th-grade girl swears by orange juice to keep her going during long study sessions. Herb tea and even plain water can be refreshing too.

47. Even if you're not getting straight A's yet, we know you're smart enough never to do drugs of ANY kind. Drugs are the fastest way to fail school—and life.

A+ Food

These foods help you feel better, concentrate better, and learn more. What's so smart about them? They keep your energy high, build strong bones, fight infections, increase your resistance, and clean your cells.

cheese

fresh fruit

whole wheat bread

turkey

water-packed tuna fish

pasta, rice, potatoes

herb tea

nuts

water

yogurt

extra-lean hamburger

broccoli

eggs

Failing Food

These foods may sound delicious, but they zap your energy, make you fat, and lower your immune system by depleting vitamins.

donuts

soda

potato chips

coffee

sugar-coated cereal

candy

white bread

hot dogs

deep-fried anything

cakes and cookies

48. Do take your prescription medicine for a chronic condition such as asthma or diabetes. It's pretty hard to get straight A's while wheezing!

49. You're going to love this tip: DO NOT WRITE any term papers, book reports, or other assignments when you're not feeling well. Unless you have no choice, do important work only when you're in tip-top shape—well rested, clear-minded, and healthy. When you have a cold or are tired, you won't do your best A+ work. If you feel as if you're always tired, get a complete checkup. Maybe you have allergies or anemia. If the doctor can't find any physical reasons for your fatigue, consider the possibility that you may be suffering from stress or depression. Depression and stress, especially in young people, can be disguised as tiredness. No one can get straight A's while depressed. So see a counselor or talk to your parents about getting help as soon as possible.

50. Many straight-A students say that exercise isn't just helpful, it's absolutely essential. Your brain runs more efficiently if you run your body regularly. Pick sports you enjoy so you'll keep it up. Think you're not athletic? Try:
- Dancing to your favorite music
- Walking your dog
- Flying a kite
- Skateboarding
- Rollerblading
- Swimming

51. Get enough sleep! Figure out how much sleep your mind needs to be its sharpest. Everyone is different, so you have to experiment. Any of the following signs means you might need more sleep:

- You're still tired when you first wake up in the morning.
- You're cranky almost all the time.
- You fall asleep in class.
- You fall asleep instantly when your head hits the pillow—or the back of the chair in assembly.

52. If you suspect you'd get better grades if you got more sleep, try going to bed 15 minutes earlier each week until your sleepiness goes away.

53. Change a light bulb! Believe it or not, what kind of light you use can affect your grades. Researchers compared different types of lighting on 10- to 12-year-olds at five schools. They discovered that students whose classrooms had full-spectrum fluorescent bulbs learned more than students who spent their time under cool-white fluorescent lighting. Unfortunately, most American schools use the cool light bulbs. But you might want to try talking to your teachers or principal about changing.

54. Make sure your classrooms, bedrooms, and anywhere else you try to study aren't overheated or freezing cold. It's hard to learn if you feel as if you're sitting in a tropical rainforest or on top of an iceberg.

YOU AND STRESS

Sometimes you don't realize how much stress you're under until your body tells you by getting sick. Once you're sick, it's much harder to get good grades in school. This chart, adapted from one for adults, rates stressful events on a scale of 1-100. You may be surprised to see that even fun, positive experiences can cause stress. Adding up your stress score will give you a hint as to how much stress might be affecting your body and brain. If your score is high, you might want to keep a low profile for awhile and take extra good care of yourself. You might also talk to your parents, a teacher, or guidance counselor.

Event	Stress score
Divorce of parents	73
Death of a family member	63
Major illness or injury	53
Major change in family member's health	44
New family member (through birth or adoption)	39
Death of a close friend	37
Outstanding achievement	28
Starting or stopping school	26

Event	Stress score
Change in housing (remodeling or building)	25
Change in how you dress, behave, manners	24
Trouble with teachers or parents	23
Moving	20
Changing to a new school	20
Major change in type and amount of recreation	19
Change in sleep (a lot more or a lot less)	16
Change in usual number of family get-togethers	15
Change in eating habits	15
Vacations	13
Christmas	12
Breaking minor laws (traffic tickets, jaywalking)	11

CHAPTER 6

You and Your Teachers: Pet or Pet Peeve?

55. Most teachers welcome the chance to explain their subjects—that's why they became teachers! They want you to learn too. Ask for extra help after class, during lunch, or before school.

56. Do a little bit more than the teacher asks you to do. Read ahead in your textbook, do a few more math problems, add an illustration to a report. A few minutes of extra effort really adds up!

57. Teachers want to see that you're interested in learning, not just getting good grades. As one successful high schooler told us, "Don't be a grade grub! Don't just ask how can I get an A in your class? Instead, say how can I get the most out of your class? Or learn the most?"

58. Every EXTRA little bit helps. Say you've been sailing smoothly through a semester in social studies, getting nothing but A's on every test and report. Towards the end of school, your soccer team is in the playoffs. You are preoccupied, have no time to study, and blow the final test. Does that mean your straight-A average is blown too? Not if you've done EXTRA CREDIT! Doing extra credit assignments is like putting quarters in the report card bank. Ask your teachers how you can earn extra credit.

59. Try to figure out what your teacher wants. This might sound simple, but most teachers don't like to come right out and tell you. So you have to be a bit of a detective. Does she like to give long lectures on one subject? Chances are she'll want your papers to be based on facts. Does she encourage loose class discussions? Then maybe she'll appreciate a more personal approach in book reports.

60. ALWAYS do homework. It counts! Teachers put a lot of time and effort into homework assignments. A test grade average in the 80s can become an A if your homework grades are high! If you MUST turn in homework late—for a good reason such as absence—give it to your teacher BEFORE you're asked for it.

61. You've heard the old expression *Don't judge a book by its cover*—but teachers sometimes *do* grade on appearances. In other words, neatness counts! So do your homework assignments and essays neatly, on lined paper with no rips or stains.

62. Use a computer to really score points with teachers. Computers make your reports easier to read, easier to spell-check, easier to edit, and they leave you more time to perfect your paper.

63. Show up on time for class. Otherwise you risk annoying the teacher, missing crucial facts, or getting too flustered to pay attention. Do whatever it takes, whether it's wearing a watch, setting your alarm earlier, or running instead of strolling.

64. Try to participate in class without taking over. Offering a good guess if you don't know the answer is almost always better than never raising your hand. Ask lots of questions. Act self-confident. You'll save yourself hours of time struggling to grasp a concept you don't understand if you ask right away. If shyness is a problem, practice questions in advance. Set a goal of asking one question or making one comment per class.

65. Answer questions in class in complete sentences, not just mumbled phrases. For example, if your teacher asks, "Do you think the President is doing a good job?" an average student might answer, "Yeah, I guess..." while a straight-A student will say, "Yes, I think the President is doing a very good job because in the last two years he has kept us out of war, lowered taxes, and gotten important laws passed."

66. Smile! Teachers love to look out at a sea of shining happy faces. Usually what they see is more like an ocean of grim-looking fish. If you smile, you'll really stand out.

67. Make eye contact with your teacher. It will help your teacher notice you AND help you listen more carefully to whatever the teacher is saying.

68. Pay attention to the way you communicate without words to your teacher. Do you slouch or sit up straight in class? Do you moan or sigh loudly whenever the teacher gives a homework assignment or announces a quiz? These "nonverbal" clues can affect the grade your teacher thinks you deserve.

69. Think of each new teacher as your chance for a fresh start. Forget past marks or mistakes. Use the opportunity of a new year to make a terrific impression.

Questions Teachers Love to Hear . . .
and Straight-A Students Ask a Lot

- How can I learn how to *think* and not only memorize?
- I'm having trouble understanding this section. Could you please explain it?
- I'd like to learn more about this subject. Can you give me some extra reading suggestions?
- How can I get a little extra credit?
- What would you say is the best way to study for this test?
- I'd like to do well in your class. Could you tell me my strengths and weaknesses in this subject?
- When is the best time to talk to you outside class?
- How did you become interested in teaching (*fill in the subject*)?

Excuses Teachers Never Like to Hear . . .
and Straight-A Students
Would Never Use

- I just hate (*fill in the subject*—at your own risk.)
- I forgot.
- I didn't have time.
- I'm too busy.
- I had a game.
- I didn't think I needed to.
- I had a date.
- I had a play.
- It fell out of my backpack on the way to school.
- I must have left it at home.
- My dog . . . you know the rest.

CHAPTER 7

You and Your Parents: They're On Your Side!

70. How well do you know your parents? Do you know what they majored in at college? What they do now for a living? What their favorite hobbies are? Parents can be great resources and helpers—but only if you know what to ask them!

71. Be clear about your parents' expectations of you as a student. Do they want you to get straight A's? Do they set high standards for you? It may be hard to do well in school if your parents are either too pushy or too lax. Talk it out with them.

72. Ask your parents for specific help in your weaker subjects. One middle-schooler was having a slump in science. His mom asked him to show her all his tests and homework. Together they figured out that his problem was not understanding graphs. She showed him how to read a graph. His grade went up!

61

73. Tell your parents you want them to keep you on track. If they see you wandering around the house, for example, humming the latest hit song, they can gently but firmly tell you to finish your homework before you fantasize about being the next big rock star.

74. Teach your parents! Teaching a subject to someone else reinforces your knowledge and helps you get a better grade.

75. If you do well when your parents reward your good grades, go for it. Ask them to give you special treats that will make you work harder. Maybe an end-of-the-year trip to your favorite amusement park or tickets to a rock concert is your ticket to straight A's.

76. Some students feel stressed when their parents make too big a deal over their grades. If that's you, politely explain to your parents that pressure doesn't help motivate you.

77. Ask your parents to spend a few minutes each day discussing school with you, if they don't already. Studies show that children of parents who take an interest in their schoolwork get better grades.

78. Watch the evening news together. Interview your parents about their opinions of what's going on in the world.

79. Request that your parents subscribe to magazines and newspapers that will help you get better grades. They can tell relatives to give the family subscriptions as gifts too. Here are a few basic periodicals a straight-A student's home should have:

- A daily newspaper
- National Geographic
- *Newsweek* or *Time*

80. The more family trips you take to art, science, or history museums, historical sites, plays, and concerts, the more your mind will be exposed to information that will help your grades in many different ways. Encourage your parents to take you on outings. Many of these places are either free or have student discounts.

81. There's nothing worse for your grades than going to school after you've had an argument with your parents. Try to avoid conflict in the morning—fight at night! Better yet, request weekly family meetings to work problems out before they turn into major distractions to getting good grades.

82. If there are problems with your parents you have no control over, try to find a quiet place to do your schoolwork: an afterschool program, study halls, a library, even a friend's house.

CHAPTER 8

You and Your Friends: Pals or Problems?

83. Think about the friends you have now. Are they the same people you hung around with in first grade? As you've grown older, maybe you've changed. Maybe it's time to make new friends whose goals are similar to yours. Sometimes a change in friends can mean a change in grades.

84. Try to make friends with the smartest students. Chances are you'll soon discover that far from being "nerds," they're fun to hang out with—and you'll learn a lot from them. You will probably be able to teach them a few things, too!

PLAYING SMART

Play games with a friend! Believe it or not, playing certain games can help you get better grades by improving your logic, vocabulary, and knowledge. Try some of these:

For increasing vocabulary
- Scrabble
- Boggle
- Dictionary
- Taboo

For general knowledge
- Brain Quest
- Trivial Pursuit
- Made for Trade

For strategic thinking, logic, and math
- Chess
- Risk
- 24 Game
- Yahtzee

Can you think of other games you already play that may help you learn?

85. Find a homework buddy in each of your classes. Trade phone numbers and when one of you is out sick, call each other for assignments, notes, and handouts.

86. Sit with the top students in each class, if you have a choice of where to sit. Notice what they do while the teacher is speaking. Do they look at the teacher? Take notes? Answer questions? Try to do some of these things, and you'll be more motivated to pay attention.

87. Make up practice tests and quizzes after you finish a unit. Test a friend, then have a friend test you to review for an upcoming quiz. The more you quiz yourself and others, the better your chances for getting an A.

88. Join forces with friends to ask a teacher for help or talk to the principal about a problem in school. One group of 9th grade students went to the principal because they weren't learning enough in math class. The principal took their problem seriously because if they were *all* having the same problem, it was probably the teacher's weakness. Don't assume that because you are a kid, adults don't want to hear what you have to say.

89. A little friendly competition never hurts. Several straight A students can make a game out of keeping up with other good students. After a test, get together with other students and share grades. Discuss the things each of you missed on the test, and make plans to match or beat the top grade.

90. Someday, somehow, you're going to wind up in a class with an ex-boyfriend, ex-girlfriend, or a best friend with whom you just had a huge fight. Do you glare at this person for an hour and miss everything the teacher is saying? Do you plot ways to get revenge for all the things the person has ever done to you? Of course not! You "turn off" your personal life for the time you're in that class so that you can do as well in school as always.

CHAPTER 9

You and a Few Others: How to Get All Kinds of Help From All Kinds of People

91. An older brother or sister, or an older friend or neighbor who does well in school, is a great person to ask for help, especially in subjects they know better than your parents. And they're usually cheaper and more convenient than a tutor!

92. Go to the library often. Get familiar with how to find things quickly. Then when it's time to write that history paper, you'll have a head start.

93. Get to know your librarians, both in school and in the best public library near you. Find out the librarian's name. Introduce yourself to the librarian. Librarians are resourceful and their job is to help students get information. Catch them during slow times of their work day and they'll be much more willing to give you time than if you try interrupting them during a busy Saturday afternoon rush. Don't forget to be polite and respectful!

94. Tutors can really make a difference in your grades. Almost everyone learns best one-on-one. You can look for a tutor in the classified section of your local paper. For a less expensive tutor, try to find a high-school or college student who knows a subject AND knows how to teach it.

95. You might be too old to have a baby-sitter. If you aren't, take advantage of it! One boy we know learned algebra in second grade by watching his baby-sitter do her homework.

96. Your guidance counselor is a great resource. He or she can talk out personal problems so you can concentrate on your grades.

97. Go to your guidance counselor if your principal seems too intimidating. That's what four girls in an English class did when their teacher picked on them. The guidance counselor held a meeting with the girls and the teacher, plus spoke privately with the teacher. He soon stopped his unfair behavior.

You and Computers

Think of the computer as one of your best school friends. Computers can help you write reports, create graphs and charts, check spelling, grammar, and punctuation, hyphenate words correctly, teach you whole new subjects or tutor you in weak areas, and, of course, play games with you.

Online computer services contain huge amounts of reference material, advice, and humor. You can find another person online with similar interests and round out your education electronically! Here are the toll-free numbers of a few online services to get you started. (Remember they cost money to use and can be addictive!)

America Online
8619 Westwood Center Dr.
Vienna, VA 22182
1-800-827-6364

Compuserve
5000 Arlington Centre Blvd.
PO Box 20212
Columbus, OH 43220
1-800-554-4079

Prodigy
445 Hamilton Ave.
White Plains, NY 10601
1-800-776-3449

98. Guidance counselors can refer you to summer or weekend enrichment programs, tutors, and other specialists.

99. Guidance counselors often give study skills courses. Check with your school.

100. The best coaches want you to score in school as well as on the football field, tennis court, or track. If you feel your sports practices are keeping your grades down, talk to your coach immediately. In the big picture, an A is going to get you further in life than winning the game.

101. Look for experts in various fields among your family friends, neighbors, church members, scout leaders—everywhere! They'd love to share their special knowledge with an enthusiastic person like you. And flexing your brain, like flexing any muscle, will make it stronger.

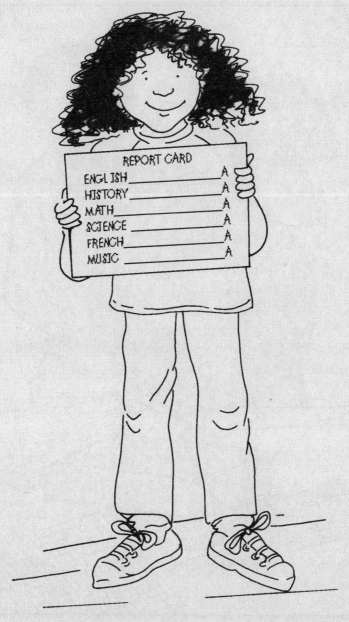

CHAPTER 10

Resources and References

Supplies You Must Have to Get Straight A's

Elements of Style, Strunk and White. This is the shortest, coolest, best little book ever written on how to write. For example, do you get mixed up between effect and affect, then and than, further and farther? Strunk and White have the answers. Keep a copy on your desk, in your locker, in your backpack—wherever you will be doing any writing.

An unabridged dictionary *(Not* a "college" or "student" dictionary. Some to look for: American Heritage, Random House, Webster's). Browse through it in a free moment. Learn one new word a day.

Roget's International Thesaurus (If you don't know what a thesaurus is, look it up in your dictionary. Of course you now have a dictionary.)

An atlas
A globe or large world map
   for quick, easy reference
graph paper for
   math problems

pencil sharpener
assignment pad
stapler
paper clips
pocket folder for each subject

calculator to check math
    problems
Wite-Out to clean up
    mistakes
index cards
pens and pencils

highlighter
library card
alarm clock
phone list of homework pals
    (one for each class)

Lost in Reference

Remember the fantastic, free resources awaiting you at your nearby public library: videos, compact discs, books on tape, computer databases, magazines, poetry readings, and more. Try using some of the following for your next report. Bet you'll get an A!

Almanacs
An almanac is updated every year with different lists, charts, and tables of information.
Information Please Kids' Almanac, Guinness Book of World Records, Farmers' Almanac, World Almanac and Book of Facts

Biographical Dictionaries
These dictionaries are like mini-encyclopedias with descriptions of famous people in various fields.
Current Biography, Who's Who, Contemporary Authors, Dictionary of American Biography

Directories and Guidebooks
Lists of institutions, organizations, places, and other useful information.
Barron's Top Fifty: An Inside Look at America's Best Colleges, Guide to Summer Camps & Summer Schools, Fodor's Travel Guides

Dictionaries, Specialized

Dictionaries that contain only definitions of a certain family of terms. They are fun to skim for ideas on research papers or essays.

Oxford English Dictionary, Dictionary of Quotations, Dictionary of Music, Dictionary of Synonyms and Antonyms, Misspeller's Dictionary

Encyclopedias

Reference works that usually consist of many volumes and contain short articles on a wide range of subjects. Encyclopedias can be found on computer online services too.

World Book Encyclopedia, Collier's Encyclopedia, Encyclopaedia Britannica, Encyclopedia Americana

Gazetteers

Dictionaries or indexes of geography.

Hammond, An A-Z of Geographical Information, Chambers World Gazetteer

Manuals

Instruction reference guides.

The Chicago Manual of Style, Manual for Writers of Term Papers, Theses & Dissertations

Dewey Decimal System

Your yellow brick road to the Land of the Library. This is the way books are numbered so you can find them more easily. Look for the numbers on the spine of each book as well as on the ends of bookcases.

000-099 General works (Encyclopedias, magazines, almanacs, bibliographies)
100-199 Philosophy, psychology, ethics
200-299 Religion and myths
300-399 Sociology (civics, economics, education)
400-499 Philology (language, dictionaries, grammar)
500-599 Science (math, chemistry, biology, botany)
600-699 Useful arts (medicine, agriculture, television)
700-799 Fine arts (painting, music, photography)
800-899 Literature (novels, poetry, plays)
900-999 History, geography, biography

Prefixes

Don't leave home without knowing these prefixes. They expand your vocabulary instantly, give you a step-up when you have to guess definitions on standardized tests, and help reading comprehension. Plus, prefixes are fun!

ab-	away from	abnormal, absorb
bi-	two	biannual, biceps
dis-	not	disenchant, disgrace
ex-	out of	exclude, exempt
in-	into	inside, infest
in-	not	incurable, independent
mis-	wrong	misbehave, misplace
post-	after	postbellum, posterior
pre-	before	prenatal, preview
re-	again	review, reunite
re-	back	reverse, revive
sub-	under	subjacent, submit
trans-	across	transatlantic, transgress
tri-	three	tricycle, trident
un-	not	unequal, uneven

SYNONYMS AND OTHER -ONYMS

Knowing the meanings of synonym, antonym, and homonym can help you do better on standardized tests. Knowing what these other -*onym* words mean is just plain fun! By the way, the suffix -*onym* means *name*.

Acronym A word formed from the first letters of a group of words or names. EXAMPLE: *yuppie* (young urban professional).

Antonym A word with the opposite meaning of another word. EXAMPLE: the antonym of *cold* is *hot*.

Capitonym A word that has a different meaning if capitalized. EXAMPLE: *catholic, Catholic.*

Charactonym The name of a character that also describes the person. EXAMPLE: *Puck* in Shakespeare's *A Midsummer Night's Dream* is a mischievous sprite.

Eponym A word from the name of a person. EXAMPLE: *braille* from Louis Braille, the inventor of the writing system for the blind.

Heteronym A word that is spelled like another word but has a different meaning when pronounced differently. EXAMPLE: *lead* (to conduct), *lead* (the metal).

Homonym A word that is pronounced the same as another word but means something different. EXAMPLE: *son* (a child), *sun* (the star).

Pseudonym A made-up name an author uses. EXAMPLE: *Dr. Seuss* was the pseudonym of Theodore Geisel.

Synonym A word that has the same meaning as another word. EXAMPLE: a synonym for *autumn* is *fall*.

Toponym A word that comes from the name of a place. EXAMPLE: *frankfurter* from Frankfurt, Germany.

THE THREE BRANCHES OF THE UNITED STATES GOVERNMENT

Legislative

CONGRESS
SENATE   HOUSE OF REPRESENTATIVES
Architect of the Capitol
U.S. Botanic Garden
General Accounting Office
Government Printing Office
Library of Congress
Office of Technology Assessment
Congressional Budget Office
Copyright Royalty Tribunal
U.S. Tax Court

Executive

PRESIDENT
VICE PRESIDENT   CABINET
EXECUTIVE OFFICE OF THE PRESIDENT
White House Office
Office of Management and Budget
Council of Economic Advisors
National Security Council
Office of Policy Development
Office of the U.S. Trade Representative

Council on Environmental Quality
Office of Science and Technology Policy
Office of Administration
Office of National Drug Control Policy
National Critical Materials Council
National Space Council

Judicial

SUPREME COURT OF THE UNITED STATES
Court of Appeals
District Court
Claims Court
Court of Appeals for the Federal Circuit
Court of International Trade
Territorial Court
Court of Military Appeals
Court of Veteran Appeals
Administrative Office of the Courts
Federal Judicial Center

Do You Get A's in Spelling Bees?

The Scripps Howard National Spelling Bee is for students in eighth grade or lower. Each year finalists compete in Washington, D.C. for the top prizes. Could you have spelled these winning words? Do you know what they mean?

1993 kamikaze	1983 Purim	1973 vouchsafe
1992 lyceum	1982 psoriasis	1972 macerate
1991 antipyretic	1981 sarcophagus	1971 shalloon
1990 fibranne	1980 elucubrate	1970 croissant
1989 spoliator	1979 maculature	1969 interlocutory
1988 elegiacal	1978 deification	1968 abalone
1987 staphylococci	1977 cambist	1967 chihuahua
1986 odontalgia	1976 narcolepsy	1966 ratoon
1985 milieu	1975 incisor	1965 eczema
1984 luge	1974 hydrophyte	

Summer Enrichment Programs

Pre-College Program
American University's
  Washington Semester
Tenley Campus
The American University
Washington, DC 20016
800-424-2600

Bennington July Program
Bennington College
Bennington, VT 05201
802-442-5401

Exploration Summer
  Program
Wellesley College
124 High Rock Lane
Westwood, MA 02090
617-320-9179

Horace Mann Summer
  Programs
231 West 246th St.
Bronx, NY 10471
718-548-4000

Center for Talented Youth
Johns Hopkins University
3400 No. Charles St.
Baltimore, MD 21218
410-516-0667

National High School
  Institute
Northwestern University
2299 North Campus Dr.
Evanston, IL 60208
800-662-NHSI

Tufts College Experience
108 Packard Ave.
Medford, MA 02155
617-627-3568

Helpful Organizations

Gifted Child Society, Inc.
190 Rock Rd.
Glen Rock, NJ 07452

National Association for Gifted Children
4175 Lovell Rd.
Circle Pines, MN 55014

MENSA Gifted Children Program
5403 1st Place North
Arlington, VA 22203

Children with Attention Deficit Disorders
499 NW 70th Ave. Suite 308
Plantation, FL 33317

Learning Disabilities Association of America
4156 Library Road
Pittsburgh, PA 15234

Recorded Books, Inc.
270 Skipjack Road
Prince Frederick, MD 20678
800-638-1304

Bibliography

Aaseng, Nathan. *Florence Griffith-Joyner.* Minneapolis, MN: Lerner Publications, 1989.

Bean, Reynold. *How to Help Your Children Succeed in School.* Los Angeles, CA: Price Stern Sloan, 1991.

Beuvald, Beverly. *Sandra Day O'Connor.* New York: Ballantine, 1991.

Black, Ginger. *Making the Grade.* New York: Carol Publishing Group, 1989.

Buranelli, Vincent. *Thomas Alva Edison.* Englewood Cliffs, NJ: Silver Burdett Press, 1989.

Canter, Lee and Marlene Canter. *Homework Without Tears.* New York: HarperCollins, 1987.

Colman, Penny. *101 Ways to Do Better in School.* Mahwah, NJ: Troll Associates, 1994.

Copeland, Edna and Valerie Love. *Attention, Please.* Atlanta, GA: SPI Press, 1991.

de Kay, James T. *Meet Martin Luther King, Jr.* New York: Random House, 1989.

Faber, Doris and Harold Faber. *Great Lives: Nature and the Environment.* New York: Scribner's, 1991.

Gruber, Gary. *Dr. Gary Gruber's Essential Guide to Test Taking for Kids.* New York: William Morrow, 1986.

Hummel, Donna et al. *Study Guide to Accompany Child Psychology.* New York: McGraw-Hill, 1986.

Jacobs, William. *Great Lives, Human Rights*. New York: Scribner's, 1990.

Johnson, Richard L. *Magic Johnson*. Minneapolis, MN: Dillon Press, 1992.

Klavan, Ellen. *Taming the Homework Monster*. New York: Poseidon Press, 1992.

McCarthy, Laura Flynn. "Better Learning Through Better Lighting," *Family Life*, March 1994.

McCutcheon, Randall. *Get Off My Brain*. Minneapolis, MN: Free Spirit, 1985.

McLoone-Basta, Margo and Alice Siegel. *The Kids' Book of Lists*. New York: Holt, Rinehart and Winston, 1980.

McTighe, Jay. *Graphic Organizers*. Baltimore, MD: Maryland State Department of Education.

Maeroff, Gene. *The School Smart Parent*. New York: Times Books, 1989.

Naylor, Phyllis. *Getting Along With Your Teachers*. Nashville, TN: Abingdon, 1981.

Orr, Fred. *Test-Taking Power*. New York: Prentice Hall Press, 1986.

Radencich, Marguerite and Jeanne Shay Schumm. *How to Help Your Child With Homework*. Minneapolis, MN: Free Spirit, 1988.

Sardman, Anne. *Stephen King*. Minneapolis, MN: Lerner Publications, 1992.

Schumm, Jeanne Shay and Marguerite Radencich. *School Power*. Minneapolis, MN: Free Spirit, 1992.

Siegel, Alice and Margo McLoone-Basta. *The Information Please Kids' Almanac*. New York: Houghton Mifflin, 1992.

Silberman, Arlene. *Growing Up Writing: Why Johnny & Janie Can't Write and What We Can Do About It*. New York: Times Books, 1989.

Study Skills. Chicago: World Book, Volume 1, 1986.

Vacca, Richard and JoAnne Vacca. *Content Area Reading*. Glenview, Illinois: Scott, Foresman and Company, 1987.

Wikler, Janet. *How to Study and Learn*. New York: Franklin Watts, 1978.

World Almanac and Book of Facts 1994. New York: Pharos Books, 1993.

Index

Notes

Notes